Project-Based Multimedia Instruction

by
John D. Foshay

ISBN 0-87367-645-9

Bloomington, Indiana

This fastback is sponsored by the
State University College/New Paltz
Chapter of Phi Delta Kappa
International, which made a generous
contribution toward publication costs.

The chapter sponsors this fastback to
celebrate the chapter's 25th anniversary.

Table of Contents

Introduction

Today's technology enables teachers to integrate multimedia and project-based instruction. The computer hardware and software currently available in many schools allow teachers and students to incorporate high-tech text, pictures, audio, and video into classroom presentations and projects that once were restricted to using posters and papier-mâché.

Learning to make computer-based presentations no longer requires the study of complex programming languages. Instead, such software programs as HyperCard, HyperStudio, and Linkway let students and teachers design multimedia presentations using intuitive menu choices and simple mouse actions. These software programs, collectively known as "authoring programs," are the "next step" after word-processing programs. Teachers can use them to produce colorful, engaging instructional presentations; students can use them to design equally colorful and articulate presentations of their learning projects.

While computer output (text, pictures, designs) is one feature, the more advanced uses of authoring programs are to create computer-based lessons (most often a teacher activity) and to design computer-based presentations (both teachers and students). The distinction between these two forms is simply interactivity. "Presentations" are most often designed to display information, albeit in more engaging ways than have been possible traditionally. "Lessons" conceived in multimedia are more often created to be interactive, so that a student engaging in the lesson can respond, for example, by answering questions, filling in information, or making choices among options. But there are more similarities than differences in developing presentations and lessons.

As would be the case in any form of instruction, the effective use of multimedia requires defining a purpose and choosing words and images — and forms of interactivity, if applicable — that will support that purpose. Lessons and presentations tend to work best when they are focused by a well-defined topic or theme. For example, a multimedia project might be designed around the theme, "Explorers." Students might choose a famous explorer or team of explorers (such as Lewis and Clark) and then do research to find out about the nature of the exploration, what the explorers' found, where they went, and so on. A presentation of the students' findings might include photographs of the explorers, text explaining their expeditions, and maps of their exploration routes.

The basis of such project-focused instruction is hardly new. Early in this century William Heard Kilpatrick, a professor at Teachers College Columbia University and a colleague of John Dewey, advocated project-based instruction. His notion was that such instruction should include four components: "purposing" (defining a purpose), planning, executing, and judging. He asserted that engaging students in purposeful activities that they help to select, plan, implement, and evaluate facilitates students' learning and helps them solve problems and acquire the skills and judgment necessary to function as adults in a democratic society (Kilpatrick 1926).

Seventy-five years later, Kilpatrick's beliefs are still current. His philosophy places the teacher in the role of learning facilitator — coach or guide — and thus thrusts the student into a role of active learner — as researcher, collaborator, author, artist, or a combination of these.

My purpose in this fastback is to provide a primer on developing project-based multimedia instruction. The information is necessarily general because many computer programs exist and schools across the nation are at very different stages in their acquisition and use of technology. However, the general principles are sound and tested, and I have attempted to focus on the practical and the doable.

Why Use Multimedia?

Perhaps the first case to be made is one for using multimedia. It probably is insufficient to posit that multimedia should be used (à la Edmund Hillary) "because it is there." In fact, apart from multimedia being nearly omnipresent (at least in some settings), there are clear advantages to be gained instructionally from teachers using multimedia and, from the standpoint of active learning, from students using multimedia.

Taking up the latter consideration first, for example, students who learn to operate a video camera are developing skills in multiple domains. Operating a video camera is a psychomotor skill involving both mental and physical activity (Dick and Carey 1996). Capturing images and sound on tape or disk requires hand-eye coordination, a sense of composition, an ear for useful sounds and dialogue, and so on.

Developing multimedia presentations also requires students to use sequencing and selection skills. They must define a concept, create a story board, apply software program rules and actions, and use an array of menu commands in order to successfully manipulate an authoring program to produce the presentation they want.

Multimedia also tend to multiply information. Students seek out facts, figures, pictures, and sounds — static images and moving images — and must discriminate among the many pieces of information they find, keeping and discarding with care. Then, using the mass of information that is left, they must organize it into a rich, cohesive presentation. All of this relates admirably to higher-level thinking, precisely what most teachers want from their students.

Three theoretical constructs are readily evident in multimedia use. For example, using multimedia engages many *learning styles*. Students who learn best by reading will find much to read in text found in books, online, or in disk-based technology. Students who learn best from graphic or visual representations will find those in abundance. And students who learn best through hands-on activity will be engaged by the physical/visual requirements of using the authoring programs. Similarly, teachers who employ multimedia for instructional presentations, like students who develop their own multimedia projects, can scarcely avoid touching on many of the *multiple intelligences* — verbal/linguistic, visual/spatial, etc. — identified by Howard Gardner. And, third, use of multimedia is readily incorporated in a *constructivist teaching* approach that taps students' prior knowledge and calls on them to integrate new schema with existing understandings. (For more detailed information about these instructional approaches, see the following fastbacks: 342 *Teaching for Multiple Intelligences*, 384 *Strategies for Educating Diverse Learners*, and 390 *Constructivist Teaching*.)

According to D'Ignazio (1992), using multimedia facilitates such practices as cooperative learning, group problem solving, critical thinking, reflection, analysis, inquiry, process writing, and public speaking. Activities found in multimedia development include conducting research, making content outlines and storyboards, finding pictures, creating sounds, and recording video clips, all of which foster examination and re-evaluation of goals during the work. Thus the creation of instructional multimedia presentations is inherently metacognitive.

Multimedia presentations also enhance teaching. The education literature is rich with articles written by teachers describing their work to implement instructional multimedia lessons. According to Carver, Howard, and Lan (1996), for example, creating multimedia presentations provides interesting learning experiences for unmotivated students. Multimedia lessons also help to engage learners from culturally diverse backgrounds (Smith 1992) and to provide greater learning opportunities for students with disabilities (Monohan and Susong 1996). Fredrickson (1997) also demonstrates how multimedia lessons can encourage students to create research reports and presentations with respect for their local culture and "local flavor."

The Panel on Educational Technology, created in 1995 under the President's Committee of Advisors on Science and Technology, studied applications of various technologies in K-12 education in the United States. Based on research literature and White House briefings from university and business researchers, practicing educators, software developers, and government agencies and organizations related to technology and education, the panel made several recommendations. Two of these recommendations are pertinent for inclusion in this fastback, because they address emphases that need to be understood in the context of questioning why to use multimedia. The panel posited a focus on instruction to which technology would be subservient. Their recommendations include:

- Focus on learning *with* technology, not about technology; and
- Emphasize content and pedagogy, not just hardware. (President's Committee 1997, emphasis added).

The emphasis in the phrase, "project-based multimedia," is on the first part, providing project-based instruction. "Multimedia" is the support — often the enabler — for such instruction.

How Authoring Programs Work

At the risk of contradicting the dictum to learn with, not about, technology, I would suggest that it is necessary to acquire at least a rudimentary understanding of how authoring programs, in general, work. This is knowledge at the application level, however, not at the technical level.

All authoring programs are based on the premise that the user (the "author") will create a presentation that will be displayed on a computer screen. Most programs also are designed to be able to produce some form of hard copy, usually text or pictures. But the true advantage of authoring programs — the multimedia advantage — is their capacity to display various types of images, static and moving, in sequence and simultaneously and, if desired, to engage the viewer interactively.

Authoring programs force consideration of two roles: user, or audience, and developer. As users (viewers/listeners) of television, for example, we may be only peripherally aware of camera angles, microphones, lights, and background sounds that create the scene before us on the television screen. We are affected by the totality of the presentation. But as developers we become director and crew "behind the scenes," so to speak. Like programmers for an automatic teller machine (ATM), we must decide which buttons activate which responses — disbursement of currency, display of onscreen messages — all of which the user can take for granted, content merely to smile as the screen displays, "Thank You," and then pocket the cash and a receipt.

The job of an authoring program is to make it easy to program the ATM, to point the camera and the microphone, to create the finished production. Where once creating a multimedia presentation would have required a high degree of technical knowledge and an enormous amount of time, now teachers and students can step metaphorically into a technologically enhanced "studio" and create a vibrant, effective multimedia presentation in a matter of minutes or hours, rather than days and weeks.

The four main components of developing a multimedia presentation are:

- Researching subject matter;
- Writing text;
- Acquiring media; and
- Assembling the presentation.

The author's control over the final form of the presentation, however, will be tempered by the flexibility of the authoring program. For example, although an author can use similar media in both HyperCard and HyperStudio, only HyperStudio will create a link from the presentation to the World Wide Web. On the other hand, the scripting capacity of HyperCard exceeds that of HyperStudio. Thus, given some latitude to choose among authoring programs, an author may decide to use a particular program according to a need or desire to do certain things.

Space does not permit a full description of the various features of individual authoring programs. Rather, it will be productive, by way of introduction, simply to describe how authoring programs work in general. The most commonly available programs — among them, HyperCard, HyperStudio, and Linkway — follow a "cardstack" approach. This is an apt metaphor. The author creates "cards" (or "screens") of information and then decides an order in which to "stack" them.

Each card is a page display, or "screen," of information. A card may contain one or more media: text, static photographs or graphics, videos, animation, sound, and so on.

A stack is a group of related and linked cards. The relationship may be thematic. For example, all of the cards might relate to the theme, "Explorers." All of the Explorer cards will be linked to one another. That is, when a "button" on one screen, or card, is activated, then another screen related to the first one is displayed. Linkage may be sequential. In other words, the first screen will link to the second, the second to the third, and so forth.

An example might be a stack on the theme, "Social Effects of Assembly-Line Production." The first card might deal with information about the beginnings of assembly-line production. That card might lead to a second screen of examples, perhaps containing photographs of early assembly lines or a silent newsreel film clip. From this screen the viewer might go to a third screen, highlighting social and economic effects of assembly-line production. A fourth screen might take the viewer to an early Ford automobile factory and an in-depth look at the ramifications of Ford's pioneering work in assembly-line technology.

However, linkage does not have to be sequential. In other words, the "stacks" can be ordered in many different ways. In the previous example, this might mean that the viewer could begin with the in-depth look at Ford, then go to social and economic effects generally, bounce to the beginnings of assembly-line production, and end up at the multiple examples screen. Another viewer could tackle the stack in a different order.

A teacher might take this nonlinear quality a step further by using "branching" as a means of moving through related screens. A simple example of the branching concept is to think of a multiple-choice test. If a student chooses answer A, a wrong answer, a new screen provides information to correct the student's misunderstanding and presents a new choice of responses. If a student chooses answer B, a correct answer, then a new screen offers new information, positive reinforcement, and new choices. Answer C leads in a different direction, as does answer D. Thus each answer branches off in a different set of directions that may, or may not, later converge.

One way to better understand linear and nonlinear stacks and branching is to explore several websites and to look at site maps for ideas that can be adapted for use in lessons and student presentations. The ability to move in many directions through various media is known as *hypermedia*. Wishnietsky defines hypermedia as "an integrated electronic environment" wherein "users can explore information about a subject or subjects using several technologies at the same time" (1992, p. 8). (A useful primer is fastback 339 *Hypermedia: The Integrated Learning Environment*.)

Moving from card to card in a stack, whether a simple stack or a large, complex stack, is a key feature of any multimedia presentation. This movement is called *navigation*. Thinking about how a user or viewer will navigate through a stack must shape all four of the development components, not just the final assembly of the presentation. The author will need to consider aspects of navigation in choosing items to include from research, in writing the text (or multiple texts), and in selecting media that best convey the necessary content.

Another aspect of navigation is whether to make linkages visible or invisible. In authoring programs the term, *button*, refers to a link-activation device. A button may be self-evident (pushbutton icon, arrow, underlined word or phrase), or it may be hidden. For example, a button might be hidden in an answer: Choose the answer and a link automatically is made. Another example might be to use invisible buttons connected to vocabulary words. When the student selects a word, the button is activated and an audio clip pronounces the word or a screen appears with the definition. Taking this aspect of navigation into account will also be necessary to plan an effective multimedia presentation.

In summary, authoring programs allow authors to control the media they want to use, from selection to arrangement. Authors create their own schematics for organizing stacks of cards, from simple linear linkages to nonlinear and branched linkages, and use an authoring program's features to create the kind of presentation that will best serve their purpose.

Designing Multimedia Projects

What must teachers do before implementing project-based instruction with multimedia? Three forms of preliminary assessment are useful. These include assessing the content to be conveyed, the technology to be used, and one's own level of expertise.

Content Assessment

The choice of content, often dictated or limited by a set curriculum, also must take into account the availability of information. And, in terms of instruction with multimedia, the question must be asked: Will this content best be conveyed using multiple media? In other words, is the topic of instruction suited to expression in visual form (still pictures, videos), audio form, or interactivity, such as through the use of an interactive, computer-based learning program. Furthermore, in a multifaceted project, the teacher must consider which parts of the project are best suited to the particular media. When should students be passive receivers of information? When should they be actively interacting with content? And when should they become presenters of information, perhaps creating performances or demonstrations in which they use multimedia?

Technology Assessment

Any successful design for instruction that uses multimedia must take into consideration the media to be used. The teacher must assess, first, whether the desired technology is available and, second, what skills will be needed to manage the technology effectively. Both hardware and software will need to be considered.

In many schools there also is the matter of scheduling, which must be carefully orchestrated. For example, if several computers are needed for a particular project, it may be necessary to schedule the availability of a mobile computer bank (which can be temporarily installed in a classroom) or, more likely, class access to a computer laboratory for a set of class periods. The teacher may need to review checkout procedures and schedules for other, one-of-a-kind items, such as digital cameras, electronic scanners, and so on. The logistics of obtaining necessary hardware and compatible software can be a major part of successfully implementing project-based instruction with multimedia.

Self-Assessment

Finally, it will be important for the teacher to assess his or her own technology skills. While few teachers would select content with which they are unfamiliar, in the rapidly developing field of multimedia technology it is easy for a teacher to be caught short by unfamiliar equipment or software programs. Therefore, a key to success will be assessing one's competence and comfort level with regard to the media components that will be integral to instruction in the project.

A further step in this self-assessment is to determine what technological skills — in addition to project content — will be needed by students and who can best provide such instruction. In most cases teachers can become quickly competent in the use of most classroom technology; however, some multimedia equipment or computer programs are sufficiently complex that it can be useful to schedule a time for a specialist to provide instruction. This is especially the case in projects in which students will take an active role in using technology for presentations or demonstrations.

At minimum, most teachers will need to be familiar with one or more authoring programs to a level that will allow them to teach their students how to use the programs and to trouble-shoot when routine problems or questions arise.

Finally, the teacher must consider how content and technology will be merged in the process. Should students be expected to work singly? In pairs? In cooperative groups? How will students interact with various media? Which students will need maximum freedom and which will need greater structure and direction? And, of course, the teacher must ask: What role will I play? When will direct instruction be appropriate? And when will the students benefit more from "guide on the side" facilitation?

The Authoring Process

Using the previous assessments as a basis, the next step is to design the project. In general this process begins with the development of a content outline.

What goals and objectives are to be met through the project? These should be the first consideration (Fitzgerald, Bauder, and Werner 1992). When they are determined, they will serve to guide the development of the content outline, which may take one of a variety of forms. For example, in the Brentwood School (described in the Sample Projects section later), the teacher created a form to guide students' writing, which served as the content outline for the project. The content outline in the Tuba City School project centered on a Navajo story. And in the Suncrest Elementary School project content was structured around interviews and text-based research.

Thus a content outline will be shaped by the ideas to be included in the project and by how those ideas will be explored and how the explorations will be organized and reported. Initial teacher responsibilities will be selecting and stating goals and objectives, choosing (and learning, if necessary) an authoring program, locating and managing reference materials, and helping students choose their own learning objectives, content, and approaches to learning within the project context.

One central aspect of any instructional design will be presentation. This aspect will affect the teacher (as presenter of information and instruction) and the student (as presenter, or demonstrator, of new knowledge and understandings). The authoring process can be linear or nonlinear, as I indicated in the previous section. Therefore, a good beginning point is to design the "stack" using a storyboard approach on paper before turning to the computer. This can save a great deal of time and frustration. A storyboard is a visual plan of presentation and can be used not only to plan how the authoring software will be used but also how media will be integrated with performance, or personal presentation, and other nonelectronic components.

A popular storyboarding technique employs 4" x 6" index cards as the templates for the screens to be stacked in the authoring program. As each screen card is designed, it can be placed on a large table. The cards can then be ordered in whatever manner seems most effective, and links can be determined. Once this paper organization is completed, the teacher or the student can transfer it into electronic form.

A variation on this technique — one that may be particularly helpful to beginners — is to substitute a standard piece of plain paper for the index card. The user draws a 6" x 8" box on the sheet to represent the computer monitor screen, and nonvisual elements (such as sounds, dialogue bites, and so on) are indicated in the margins. The margin space also is used for notes about video components, links, and other information (Ludlow, Duff, and Foshay 1998). Color coding also can help, for example, using one color for text, another color for links, and so forth. The colors make the various elements easier to see and therefore easier to translate into the authoring program.

Once the content of the screens has been determined, the next step is layout. The screen designer needs to decide how to position the elements on the screen. This process also will require the designer to acquire some elements, such as digitized pictures or artwork; to record sounds or find sound bites; and to capture or create video clips. One demand of good design is standardizing the positions of some elements, so that the stack has a sense of flow. For example, link buttons should be positioned in the same place on every screen. This standardization makes it easier for the user to follow the thought-chain of the information that is presented.

When students are the designers, it is the teacher's responsibility to oversee their work and to troubleshoot. Teachers also can develop and provide model stacks.

Stack aesthetics are important. Just as careful, consistent positioning aids the flow of information, other design aspects not only will help the presentation look polished but will help it be as "user-friendly" as possible. This means avoiding clutter on the screen, such as elaborate background images, and using clearly readable type. Screens that appear to have depth tend to be more inviting than "flat" screens. One way to increase the illusion of depth is to place picture elements in frames or on a solid-color background.

In addition to the design elements, teachers need to attend to the content. Whether developing their own presentation or helping students, teachers need to be concerned with accurate information that is presented without gender or ethnic bias. It also is helpful to check text and images for age-appropriateness. And, of course, the information presented through the authoring program needs to meet the stated goals and objectives of the project. It is easy for students to become enamored of flashy electronic "tidbits" that are tangential or wholly unrelated to the real work at hand.

It is easy to see a blending of instruction and presentation in a project involving multimedia. Botts (1995) suggests a specific blending of the two processes. For example, background images, visual effects, and icons can be selected before the actual design gets under way, thereby offering a skeleton framework on which to hang the visuals, texts, and sounds that will offer the project information. This is a kind of style-before-substance approach. But for students this approach helps to ensure stylistic continuity that, in turn, will foster informational continuity as the presentation is built during the learning process.

Time, Tests, and Trial Runs

Another key consideration for the teacher in structuring the development of a multimedia project is scheduling. What I mean goes beyond making certain that a computer lab is available, though that also is a necessary part of scheduling. In fact, the entire project should be outlined on a master schedule. What time will be given to direct instruction? To teacher presentation? To student research? To interactivity? To student storyboarding? To using the authoring program?

An important part of this schedule will be time to test the completed program, to perform one or more trial runs of the multimedia presentation. Each student or design group of students will want to test their product on their own. But an important next step can be a trial run with other students. This activity is done most usefully with a small peer group. The peer group can provide feedback to the designer(s) about accuracy, interactivity, attractiveness, clarity, and so forth. After such a trial run, the designer(s) can revise the presentation by adjusting the choice of images or text.

Clearly, this process is one of formative evaluation, both for the teacher and for the students. Way back in 1926, W.H. Kilpatrick conceived of the authoring process as a series of stages, termed *purposing, planning, executing,* and *judging.* This simple, four-stage sequence still is a useful guide, though Kilpatrick could hardly have imagined the multimedia projects of which students and teachers are capable today.

More recently, Ferretti and Okolo (1996) amplify this sequence by suggesting some additional considerations. They recommend, for example, that teachers take a guiding role in helping students to select multimedia design projects to ensure that the students' choices contain sufficient richness to engage the students for the duration of the project.

Ferretti and Okolo also recommend high teacher involvement to ensure that resources are available. They encourage teachers to be willing to sacrifice curriculum breadth for depth, so that students can delve deeply into their chosen subject matter. They also suggest that controversial topics can offer students opportunities to study multiple perspectives and will stimulate dialogue and increase motivation.

Finally, because multimedia projects are labor-intensive, Ferretti and Okolo advocate approaching them as cooperative learning activities, wherein groups, rather than individuals, tackle the complexity. Cooperative learning provides a framework that requires students to be mutually supportive so that all of the students in the group can experience success.

Acquiring Media Files

I would be remiss if I did not describe the acquisition of media files. Where does one find the images and sounds to incorporate into a multimedia presentation? And how does one go about doing so?

From the start, it will be important for teachers to remember that many images, sound bites, video clips, and so on, are protected by copyright. Although a great deal of latitude exists whereby such materials can be used for educational purposes — so-called fair use — it still is good policy to investigate the copyright status of imported materials and, when in doubt, to seek permission for use.

Fortunately, many images and such also reside in the public domain and can be used without seeking permission from a copyright holder.

Images

HyperCard, HyperStudio, and other such programs allow the user to import digitized images. Such images may be photographs, graphic designs, illustrations, or specialized lettering. The image, whether imported from an existing source or scanned into a computer program, becomes a computer file in its own right. This file can be imported into the authoring program, so that the image can be placed on one or more screens. The same is true for text files, which can be imported, copied, edited, and manipulated in various ways.

Few things in the computer world are universal. Therefore, it is important to understand file formats and which formats are compatible with the chosen authoring program. This is a matter for teacher coordination and should be given consideration in developing the project. For example, it may be helpful once a final text has been established to convert that text block into a digitized file — to treat it, in other words, as if it were a picture. In this form, it can be dropped onto any of one or more screens in the same manner that graphic elements are added to the screen.

The most common and accessible manner of acquiring media is through scanning. Scanners come in all shapes and sizes, but their basic function is the same: to take an image and create a digitized file that can be imported into an authoring program. The image may be a photograph, a map, a student's drawing, a design on a piece of fabric, and so forth. A wide range of scanning formats is available. For example, HyperStudio accepts digitized files in the following formats: PICT, TIFF, GIF, JPEG, PhotoCD, PCX, EPS, MacPaint, and QuickTime.

An alternative to scanning found images is the use of computerized "clip art." Clip art is commercially produced artwork, which is made to be used in authoring programs. Most clip art is published on compact discs;

and the images can be used by students and teachers with few, if any, restrictions. Indeed, many authoring programs contain clip art files; but these "built-in" files can be supplemented by the many available clip art CDs.

Another source of clip art is the World Wide Web. To locate clip art on the Web, the user can activate a search engine—such as Yahoo, Lycos, or Infoseek—and search for "royalty-free clip art." This search will produce sites that allow visitors to download images, though some sites may charge a fee for the privilege of doing so.

Scanned images and clip art can be supplemented by yet another source of images: digital photography. The digital camera resembles a traditional camera, except that it produces a digitized image. This image, captured in a computer file, can then be used in the same manner as an image file obtained by scanning. Digital cameras continue to improve in quality, and the prices are dropping as they become more widely available.

Once an image is acquired, by whatever means, it can be manipulated (altered, edited, "morphed") using another set of software programs, such as Adobe Illustrator, Macromedia Freehand, Adobe Photoshop, and similar programs. The results of manipulation can then be imported into the authoring program.

Sounds

Sounds form a major component of multimedia projects, and they are acquired in much the same way that images are collected. Compatibility between the sound file format and the authoring program is still an issue, and there are many sound formats. HyperStudio, for example, supports SNDI, SND2, System 7 Sound resources, AIFF, AIFC, WAV, MOD Sequences, and MIDI.

Most authoring programs allow the user to capture audio files within the authoring program using a microphone connected to (or built into) the computer. Students can use this microphone to record sounds, including oral presentations, dialogues, or songs. The Arroyo Elementary School project (described in the Sample Projects section) integrated students' singing into its multimedia project, for example.

One trade-off that teachers (and students) must be prepared to make is accessibility at the sacrifice of quality. Sound quality is likely to be fairly poor, because the emphasis in most authoring programs is on image, not sound. And sophisticated sound programs, such as Macromedia's Sound Edit 16, which allows high-quality recording and editing, requires hardware that is out of the reach of most schools.

Prerecorded, predigitized audio files are another source of sounds for multimedia projects. As in the case of clip art, most authoring programs contain sample audio files for use in projects. Sometimes digitized audio files can be found on clip art CDs or sound clip CDs. And the World Wide Web is another source of audio files. A wide range of sounds exists in such files. They may include sound effects from phones ringing to applause or engines or voices. Typically, the developers label each individual file to identify the type of sound. Locating specific audio files, such as the voice of a famous person or the sounds of a certain animal, may involve contacting libraries, museums, or sound archives.

One way to incorporate music into a multimedia project is to use an authoring program that will interact with the computer's CD drive. This can allow the user to import portions of songs or entire audio tracks.

Animation and Videos

Moving images, often including sounds, are captured in the same ways that I have described for images and sounds. As in both previous cases, compatibility of programs is a key consideration. Once compatibility is ensured, the door is wide open.

However, it should be noted that digitized moving images, whether animation or video photography, are the most difficult media to create. Few student-developed projects will deal with such creation. The same is true for transforming videotape material into digitized files, a process that is complicated and requires fairly sophisticated equipment. On the other hand, finding and using digitized moving images (with or without sound) differs little from the processes I have described.

Authoring programs typically allow for some degree of animation in their products. Users can instruct the authoring program to move objects around the screen in predetermined paths. Motion may depict events found in the subject matter, such as planets orbiting the sun, ships sailing, or musical notes dancing. The capabilities of the authoring program typically define the use of animation, though software exists that is written specifically to create animation files.

Some authoring programs also provide commands to run external devices, such as a laser disc player. This is a supplemental medium. Most often the motion video segments from the laser disc will not appear on the computer monitor as part of the stack, but on a laser disc monitor that can be positioned near the computer during a presentation. Like converting videotape into digitized files, converting laser disc images into digitized files is too complicated for most school projects.

Authoring programs usually can run digitized video clips. A digitized video clip used in authored projects typically consists of analog footage that has been converted to digital information. Analog footage refers to VCR movies or footage captured with a camcorder. The VCR or the camcorder can be hooked into computers; and by using special software, the user can transfer the footage to a digital movie file.

This process requires several prerequisite hardware and software capabilities. The computer must accept the connection of the source of the video. Not only does the computer have to possess jacks to physically connect to the external video equipment, it also must possess a video board. A video board resides within the computer and allows the user to work with digital video. Digital video requires large amounts of both RAM and hard disk space. Video capturing software, such as Adobe Premiere, must reside on the computer. While this sounds fairly sophisticated, the necessary interfaces are becoming more common in schools each year.

Authoring programs do not capture video or allow for its editing. However, once moving images have been captured and edited, a completed video file can be imported just as a still image or a sound file can be imported into the authoring program.

Sample Projects

In this section I briefly describe several multimedia projects that may help readers gain a sense of the potential for project-based instruction using multimedia.

Arroyo Elementary School in Ontario, California

This project integrated music, communication, and African-American history (Scali 1994). Students researched the content with two teacher-selected texts that included artwork, lyrics, poetry, and biographies relating to African-American history. Although focused on the topic of slavery, the content outline examined the difficulties people from Africa had in communicating with each other while in America. These difficulties arose primarily from language differences. The language differences fostered communication that eventually rooted itself in music and instrument making.

The storyboard created from this content outline depicted the trip from Africa to America on slave ships, illustrated the historical facts of the time period, referenced songs chosen by students to include as a part of the presentation, delineated contributions made by talented African Americans to United States history, and marked placements for photographs.

Students created a HyperStudio stack to present their storyboard. The teacher recorded the students singing, and the sound files underscored the onscreen images. The multimedia presentation started with the slave ship journey and went through the Emancipation Proclamation period and into a contributions section that culminated with a speech by Thurgood Marshall.

Brentwood Elementary School in Austin, Texas

This project involved parents, teachers, and students throughout the school (Monohan and Susong 1996). Supported by a grant from the local university, this project started training educators and parents in how to use HyperStudio during the summer. These initial learners later became the "experts" and taught the next group of adult learners.

In one example from this schoolwide project, a teacher created a worksheet to help focus her students' writing during content development stages. The worksheet, a fill-in-the-blank form, guided students' research. It required students to choose an animal common in Texas wildlife — such as the porcupine, the red-tailed hawk, the gray fox, the bobcat, or the red-eared slider (a turtle) — and to respond to headings such as "description," "habitat," and "diet." Each heading led students to deeper questions. For example, the "description" section included indicators for student research with regard to their chosen animal's size, coloring, and outstanding physical characteristics. The "habitat" section included prompts to discover the animal's preferred terrain, where it lived in the United States and Texas, its migration habits, and whether the animal was on the endangered species list.

As a result of using this approach, the teacher reported that Texas wildlife "came to life during the classroom presentations." Students also presented the HyperStudio versions of their research projects at the Texas Computers in Education Associates Conference.

Cleveland Elementary School in Long Beach, California

This project involved teaching fifth-graders about constellations with the help of HyperStudio and cooperative learning groups (Drysdale 1992). Pairs of students researched a constellation of their choice, such as Cygnus or Taurus, using a teacher-made packet. The teacher, Ms. Drysdale, reported that her creation of a learning packet ensured that students would find the relevant information. But using the learning packet also gave students the opportunity of sorting through relevant and irrelevant text, taking notes, and incorporating their notes into content outlines. The students' tasks included gathering facts about the constellation, finding a picture or graphic image to include in a presentation, and describing the story behind the constellation's myth.

The mythological component served two purposes. First, students studied the Greek or Native American "character" myth associated with their constellation. This component required students to locate a graphic of the mythological figure and to document the formation story behind it. For example, to show this information the students could design a screen containing text about the formation story on one side paired with a drawing of the mythological character on the other side. The second purpose was to allow the myth to stimulate creative writing. Students invented their own myths and created artwork to complement their myths.

Finally, the students composed autobiographies as part of their presentation. These autobiographies told how they created their presentation and included pictures of themselves and personal facts.

The presentations also offered a learning experience, because the fifth-graders presented their projects to second-graders. The teacher commented later that the fifth-graders demonstrated a high degree of confidence in these presentations, and the second-graders were unusually attentive to their older peers.

Morgantown High School in Morgantown, West Virginia

Using autobiographies is common in project-based instruction with multimedia. In the central activity of this example, high school students enrolled in a Multimedia I class authored presentations about themselves using Linkway (Oughton and Reed 1998). The presentations included multimedia representations of hobbies, family members, friends, and interests.

This project also focused on the cognitive skills: knowledge acquisition, problem solving, and design. Oughton, as part of the data collection for his dissertation, engaged learners in metacognitive activities every two weeks. He asked students to write logs, to draw concept maps, and to solve problems. In the learner logs the students described the design skills they used and listed the thinking skills required for authoring tasks. The students used concept mapping to illustrate concepts and relationships between concepts while authoring. For the problem-solving segment, the students were required to choose a problem that they solved during multimedia development and to describe it.

Comments from students included: "Had to work out the idea on paper to ensure it would work"; "For my autobiography, I have to set specific tasks I want to get accomplished each class period"; "Put ideas and skills together to make the project"; '"Being able to follow through mentally and physically with an idea"; "You need to know how all the controls work"; "Every time we come here, we have to remember what we learned previously"; and "When creating a picture in Linkway, you have to think about where the objects will be placed in order to give the best effect."

Tuba City Boarding School District in Tuba City, Arizona

Navajo students in Arizona participated in this project to address culturally diverse learning styles (Smith

1992). People of Navajo descent are typically cooperative and noncompetitive, and they tend to possess schema that often are not represented on standardized test instruments. They lack school knowledge and may not be motivated by standard schooling practices. At the same time, they often have had experiences that are not addressed in commercially available teaching materials.

One anecdote in this study powerfully described the high-cooperation/low-competition phenomenon. In foot races on the reservation, the boys that are winning the race will intentionally slow down to allow others to catch up so they can finish the race together.

Given this environment, the teacher predicted that cooperative learning groups would be successful and decided that teaching Linkway also might be an effective way to overcome the inefficiency of previous instruction and to address concerns about low motivation and lack of resources.

In a series of lessons, students authored programs to develop reading and writing skills. English language (viewed as important by the school but typically regarded as a second language, rarely used in the Navajo culture) was the primary content. The teacher directed students in writing in English about aspects of local culture. For example, a student might write about the role of grandparents in the Navajo family. Later, the students also took up well-known Navajo stories and presented them in multimedia.

Laredo Middle School in Aurora, Colorado

This project studied explorers, geography, and decision making (Thorp 1995). Students began by learning the routes sailed by various explorers. Then these middle school students developed one branch of their multimedia presentation based on these facts. This branch included maps that used animation to depict the routes of the explorers.

Next, using a combination of creative thinking and decision making, the students invented a second branch. This second branch posed the question: "What if the explorer chose differently?" The students hypothesized alternative decisions and created a fictional outcome for the explorer. This activity, in turn, led to further analysis of the decision-making process and various possible outcomes.

HyperStudio was the vehicle for this project. The students made their presentations during the school's annual spring festival. The teacher reported that the students felt a sense of history coming to life as they imported pictures, maps, and animation into their programs.

Suncrest Elementary School in Morgantown, West Virginia

In this project, being developed as this fastback went to press and called "Tied to the Land," students in a West Virginia history course are studying the effects of coal on the state and its people (Moore 1998). Students are examining how the coal mining industry has affected and shaped occupations, communities, politics, and values. An additional goal of this project is to create multimedia materials that can be shared with other teachers for use in classrooms throughout the state. This sharing of information will be accomplished through the production of a CD-ROM and through the construction of a website.

Students will use research, writing, and computer skills and will interview and videotape people as a primary source of information on the history of the coal industry. Student teams are collecting oral histories, historic photographs, songs, stories, and video clips of industrial sites for use in their multimedia project.

Seeds University Elementary School in Los Angeles, California

Seeds University Elementary School, a laboratory school for the University of California at Los Angeles, implemented project-based instruction with multimedia with fourth-, fifth-, and sixth-graders (Galas 1997). These students studied science, oceanography, and marine biology through a variety of instructional methods, including multimedia projects, field trips, virtual field trips on the Internet, and teacher-centered didactic lessons using lecture and discussion.

In a large-group activity, students brainstormed questions and then broke into smaller groups to discuss research interests based on those questions. Discussions of current events led students to develop an interest in the effects of a local salt mine's proposed expansion on the nearby gray whale population. As students explored topics by reading, research, field trips, and teacher-centered lessons, they began to formulate plans for interactive technology projects.

The plans for this project included the goal of students creating multimedia simulations. When students recreated a simulated dolphin ecosystem, they had to build and connect factual information through interrelationships and associations. Galas writes: "When they explore how temperature, food supply and the numbers of predators in the environment combine to affect the dolphin's existence, the students learn about systems in science at a conceptual level, because they must understand connections and relationships if they are to construct an accurate model."

This point reiterates one of the perceived benefits of project-based instruction with multimedia. Projects of this nature allow for studies to include inquiry, analysis, synthesis, and critical thinking. This type of activity adds to committing facts to memory by extending into the application as well as the integration of ideas, concepts, and interrelationships with other factors.

Governor's Academy in Morgantown, West Virginia

High school seniors participated in a four-week, summer, residential, enrichment program at West Virginia University called the Governor's Honors Academy (Reed and Rosenbluth 1995). Students attended 30 two-hour sessions: 17 on HyperCard and 13 on researching a topic. The topic for this project focused on the following periods: the 1920s, the 1930s, 1945-59, and the 1960s. The teachers omitted the years 1940-44 in order to de-emphasize World War II. Student teams, each with three or four members, researched their period for significant events in the humanities. Students received an overview of information related to each period and an introduction to university library skills and listened to guest speakers on the effects of music, art, science, literature, and technology on the values of the period.

Students studied HyperCard's five objects: background/foreground, buttons, cards, stacks, and fields. Students received training in digitizing photos and animating graphics. They also participated in a discussion of summary versus detailed information as a cue to facilitate linking information on screen.

Students studying the 1960s, for example, found audio files of Dr. Martin Luther King, programmed HyperCard to play those files from a mouse click, and paired his voice with an onscreen picture. In a music stack from the decade of the 1960s, students programmed HyperCard to play digitized audio clips that linked music and history. For example, students related history and music by choosing songs in protest and in support of the Vietnam War. Selections included Sergeant Sadler's *Ballad of the Green Beret* and a work by Joan Baez. HyperCard also allowed students to manipulate the computer's CD-ROM drive in order to play Credence Clearwater Revival.

Time periods, as a theme or topic in which to situate the study of history and the humanities, provided a rich subject for the student-authored projects. The periods overflowed with significant events documented in text, pictures, sounds, and often in motion video.

Navigation decisions played a significant role in the development of the period stacks. Students received instruction in the creation of a home card. The home card, a main or initial screen, contained links to each of the major subheadings of the presentation. Each subsequent screen of information provided a link or button returning the user to the home card for the purpose of investigating other subheadings. For example, if a user arrived at a home card that contained links to politics, music, art, literature, and sports, the user could navigate through each of the categories at will.

University of Central Florida

Instruction using multimedia certainly is not limited to K-12 classrooms. The benefits of authoring do not diminish because students are older, as in this example, in which a University of Central Florida instructor taught HyperStudio to physical education majors (Mitchell and Hunt 1997).

The instructional goal described students developing innovative lesson plans. The multimedia assignment required written lesson plans, credits, and citations to references, materials, and products; an author autobiography section; and a video segment that demonstrated a routine or physical activity in dance or sport.

The instructor reported that students exhibited ownership of their work, a heightened amount of excitement in presenting their lesson plans, and a sense of camaraderie that resulted from sharing ideas and offering one another technical support. The instructor also observed students generating new ideas and ways to use multimedia as future physical educators.

The sample projects briefly described in this section demonstrate just a few ways that teachers and students have found to integrate computers into the curriculum.

The "Rosenfield" Project

Gwen Rosenbluth and Jim Fields — along with their students — created the "Rosenfield" project during a three-year collaboration. I interviewed Gwen Rosenbluth, a teacher of high school Advanced Placement English, on the topic of multimedia and project-based instruction. She was one-half of the team; the other half, Jim Fields, was a history teacher.

Rosenfield was created as a fictional town in order to provide a framework for interdisciplinary instruction in 20th Century American Literature, 20th Century American Studies, and the Linkway authoring program.

John Foshay: I've heard a little about the Rosenfield project, but could you tell me about it?

Gwen Rosenbluth: Rosenfield is a skeletal look at a community. Students developed a community: major economic sources in the community, major sources of business, whether it was agricultural or industrial. They arrived at a description in greater detail.

JF: Individually?

GR: In five groups, each with three or four students. Each group had its own family. Together, the class brainstormed families: working class, upper class, ethnic makeup. Students were instructed to make up a cross-section to represent the time periods.

JF: To reflect America?

GR: Yes, each group selected one family from the range of choices: Asian, African-American, Irish. . . . Students then developed scenarios for their family based on the historical events from a time period, 1900-1920, for example.

JF: Students described how the family was affected by those events, as in a historical or social context?

GR: Right, how did an Asian family get to Rosenfield? What jobs did they have in Rosenfield? Did Asians fight in World War I? How did events shape the family? For example, what was the likelihood of returning home from World War I alive? Did the soldier leave a family or wife behind if he died?

JF: So students studied the impact of history on the family?

GR: Then the 1920-1940 period and the flapper era and the Depression. We wrote a lot of letters. I found literature related to the time periods, both fiction and non-fiction.

JF: So the multimedia projects were presentations about the families.

GR: We found graphics and students told the story of the family in Linkway. On the positive side students worked cooperatively in groups and we integrated the content areas with technology. The downside was, this was 1995, and we were just getting into technology.

JF: You mean time to learn it and plan with it?

GR: Time is always a consideration, but we were learning the technology. We arranged our planning periods and made time to co-teach. Working together was a positive. We have 90-minute block scheduling, and another team of teachers working on a similar project arranged to have Independent Research, like a study hall, together for their planning.

JF: Do you have any suggestions for teachers thinking about this kind of approach?

GR: Pairing an experienced teacher with a new or less experienced teacher might help. It is a lot of work, far more than regular. Our textbook was not that full; I had to pull in other resources. But it was very exciting and stimulating; and having taught those courses for a number of years, we needed a new way to go about it. It was challenging. There was no teacher's edition!

JF: What was the student reaction?

GR: It was favorable. There were some frustrations with the technology, but it came together.

After the interview Rosenbluth commented that "technology was the glue." Studying 20th-century

American history and literature in a project such as Rosenfield could be completed without multimedia authoring. However, in using authoring, students had to reconstruct both factual information and their creative writing about the fictional families for presentation with Linkway. Rosenbluth felt this allowed for a deeper, more meaningful and elaborated learning process that actively engaged students in the material. In being "the glue," the authoring program facilitated analysis and synthesis of the content area, while simultaneously providing a mechanism to display creative and original thinking.

Making the Commitment

Learning authoring programs and procedures takes time. In fact, some teachers find it worthwhile to enroll in continuing education classes as a way of learning the various programs. And some districts may want to structure professional development opportunities around this activity or to provide support for teachers to take university classes in authoring.

Asking university students who know authoring programs well to serve as inservice instructors or technology interns in schools is another way to gain information about authoring. Such interns may also be able and willing to help teachers work with students and to assist in structuring projects using multimedia.

As some of the sample projects demonstrate, another form of collaboration is pairing or teaming teachers to develop interdisciplinary projects using multimedia. Parents also can be involved in these types of endeavors, and students will benefit from their presence. In fact, some parents may be more knowledgeable about authoring programs than the teachers, at least at first;

and they can, in turn, take on the role of teaching both teachers and students about authoring.

In summary, many students find projects involving multimedia to be stimulating, motivating activities. As such, these types of projects may result in increased learning. Projects using multimedia are no panacea, but they are a way of approaching teaching and learning that merits investigation by teachers who want to improve student learning.

Resources

Altschul, C., and Zarrow, L. "The Moving Bullseye: Preparing Students for a Career in Multimedia" *T.H.E. Journal* 25, no. 3 (1997): 58-60.

Botts, G. "Multimedia Presentations in 5 Easy Steps." *Media & Methods* 32, no. 2 (1995): 20, 77.

Carver, C.A.; Howard, R.A.; and Lan, W. "Active Student-Controlled Learning: Reaching the Weakest Students." *Liberal Education* 82, no. 3 (1996): 24-29.

Dick, W., and Carey, L. *The Systematic Design of Instruction.* New York: HarperCollins, 1996.

D'Ignazio, F. "Getting a Jump on the Future: Everything You'll Ever Need to Know About Multimedia Authoring Tools." *Electronic Learning* 12, no. 3 (1992): 30-31.

Drysdale, J. "Constellations and HyperStudio: A Great Solution to the Question of Computer Integration." *Writing Notebook: Visions for Learning* 10, no. 2 (1992): 4-6.

Ferretti, R.P., and Okolo, C.M. "Authenticity in Learning: Multimedia Design Projects in the Social Studies for Students with Disabilities." *Journal of Learning Disabilities* 29, no. 5 (1996): 450-60.

Fitzgerald, G.; Bauder, D.K.; and Werner, J.G. "Authoring CAI Lessons: Teachers as Developers." *Teaching Exceptional Children* 24, no. 2 (1992): 15-21.

Fredrickson, S. "Interactive Multimedia Storybooks: Integrating Technology into the Language Arts Curriculum." *Learning and Leading with Technology* 25, no. 1 (1997): 6-10.

Galas, C. "From Presentation to Programming: Doing Something Different, Not the Same Thing Differently." *Learning and Leading with Technology* 25, no. 4 (1997): 18-21.

Kilpatrick, W.H. *Foundations of Method: Informal Talks on Teaching*. New York: Macmillan, 1926.

Ludlow, B.L.; Duff, M.C.; and Foshay, J.D. "Use of Multimedia to Develop Supervision Skills: Designing Content Segments and Programming Interactive Formats." Paper presented at the Council for Exceptional Children's Division of Technology and Media, Atlanta, January 1998.

Mitchell, D.L., and Hunt, D. "Multimedia Lesson Plans: Help for Pre-Service Teachers." *Journal of Physical Education, Recreation and Dance* 68, no. 2 (1997): 17-21.

Monohan, S., and Susong, D. "Author Slide Shows & Texas Wildlife: Thematic Multimedia Projects." *Learning and Leading with Technology* 24, no. 2 (1996): 6-11.

Moore, V. Personal communication, 1998.

Oughton, J.M., and Reed, W.M. "The Effect of Hypermedia Development on High School Students' Knowledge Acquisition, General Problem-Solving Skills, and General Design Skills," *Journal of Educational Multimedia and Hypermedia* 7, no. 4 (1998): 333-63.

President's Committee of Advisors on Science and Technology and the Panel on Educational Technology. *Report to the President on the Use of Technology to Strengthen K-12 Education in the United States*. Washington, D.C.: U.S. Government Printing Office, March 1997.

Reed, W.M., and Rosenbluth, G.S. "The Effect of HyperCard Authoring on Knowledge Acquisition and Assimilation." *Computers in Human Behavior* 11, no. 4 (1995): 605-15.

Scali, N. "Music, Communication and African History (Literature, Writing and Art)." *Writing Notebook: Visions for Learning* 11, no. 3 (1994): 14-16.

Smith, K.J. "Using Multimedia with Navajo Children: An Effort to Alleviate Problems of Cultural Learning Style, Background of Experience and Motivation." *Reading and Writing Quarterly* 8, no. 3 (1992): 287-94.

Thorp, C. "Choices and Consequences." *Teaching Pre-K-8* 26, no. 32 (1995): 58-60.

Wishnietsky, Dan H. *Hypermedia: The Integrated Learning Environment*. Fastback 339. Bloomington, Ind.: Phi Delta Kappa Educational Foundation, 1992.